TAYLOR ELLIS

The Power of Networking Mixers

The Complete Guide to Hosting Mixers for Your Industry

This book was professionally typeset on Reedsy.
Find out more at reedsy.com

This Book Is Dedicated to My Fellow Mixer Maven "D"

Contents

1

Introduction

"Hosting a networking mixer is like orchestrating a cocktail party where business cards are the currency and connections are the cocktails."

Embarking on a return to the new home construction market marked a pivotal moment for my husband and me. After a two-year hiatus, we were not only rebranding our home-building business but also pivoting our construction style from custom homes to spec homes. This shift demanded a more assertive marketing approach, unlike the conventional 'wait-for-buyer-initiation' custom home-building model. Attending various community marketing events—Chamber of Commerce mixers, Homebuilder mixers, Realtor® Mixers—yielded little in terms of generating leads. They felt insular and lacking in potential.

Encouraged by my husband, teaming up with an industry ally we resolved to craft a mixer that would transcend these limitations and foster inclusivity within our industry. We birthed the most eagerly awaited and attended monthly upscale networking mixer in our community. And now, with my comprehensive guide, you too can create a thriving networking event tailored to your industry's needs.

However, the success of a monthly mixer hinges on partnership. The event night is a labor-intensive affair, demanding a delicate balance of responsibilities—greeting, door management, and more. I took charge as the greeter and emcee, while my industry confidante handled the door and financial logistics. Her preference for a more passive role complimented my outgoing nature. She managed the exchange of beverage tickets for business cards at the door, while I orchestrated connections among attendees.

My forte lay in putting people together, adeptly reading body language to ensure comfort and facilitate meaningful connections. As the emcee, I guided the flow of our events, fostering an environment where even the shyest attendees found their industry counterparts. This partnership, balancing our contrasting strengths, proved instrumental during our hosting tenure

2

Venue Visions

"Choosing a venue for a mixer is like finding the perfect outfit for a date—you want something trendy, comfortable, and not too loud! Trust me, picking the right spot can make or break your networking game. Have you ever tried making professional connections over a deafening beat? Not recommended!"

Venue Visions – Crafting the Perfect Mixer Setting In the world of networking mixers, venue selection sets the stage for success. Here's a breakdown to ensure your event venues are a networking haven, not a noise-filled nightmare.

Setting the Mixer Calendar Decide on the frequency: January to October is prime time, avoiding the holiday season's clash with personal and business events. Our October mixer was always highly anticipated because our mixer community knew it was the final mixer of the season and the venue was a beautiful garden patio. By the end of the season, it is time to take a breather—take November and December off, trust me, you'll appreciate the hiatus.

Time Management Matters Book venues wisely: Opt for no more than two hours per event. Factor in setup an hour before and an hour after for cleanup—plan for a four-hour window the night of the event.

Consistency is Key: Reliability breeds success. Sponsors and attendees crave consistency. A steady schedule keeps the mixers on everyone's radar.

Venue Vibes: What to Consider

1. **Trendy Spaces**: The spots everyone wants to be seen at. Upscale and attention-worthy, but it might dent your sponsorship budget.
2. **Newly Opened Places:** A hotbed for curiosity. Unexpectedly, our largest turnout happened at a freshly opened bar/grill—a magnet for intrigue.

"In our first year, we booked a mixer at a new venue in town. It had recently opened and when I called on the manager to see if he would be interested in adding our event to his schedule he jumped at the opportunity. He had heard about our mixers and was excited to be a part of them. As with most mixers, we were allotted space in this large venue with an expectation of 50-75 people. As guests started arriving it became apparent very quickly that our "mixer space" was going to be too small and we were going to overflow into the "off limits" food serving space nearby. Our portable audio system was rendered useless due to the hum of people talking and the acoustics in the building and of course there was not enough food! We survived the two hours, and our sponsors were happy with the turnout but it was a costly learning lesson because we blew our food and beverage budget in the first hour and my associate and I had to pay for the cost overruns. Our

*business card counts the next day verified that we had 150 attendees!
More than double what we planned for!"*

1. **Age of Venue:** Be mindful of offensive smells and accessibility of aged venues. They can smell old and moldy. Buildings that have not been renovated to meet State and Federal standards may not meet the accessibility standards of handicapped citizens.

2. **Comfort Factor:** Balancing seating and standing room. Remember, networking happens on the move, but ensure comfort for those seeking food and drinks.

3. **Size Matters:** Room to breathe is crucial. Consider extending to a patio for more space, especially in accommodating larger crowds.

4. **Public versus private:** As your event unfolds within the venue's bustling routine, it's crucial to create a distinct space for your mixer guests. Segregate your gathering, typically in the bar area, ensuring a clear demarcation from the venue's regular patrons. Stay vigilant when exchanging business cards for drink tickets, ensuring the alignment of attendees with the event's purpose-based.
   on the information conveyed by their business cards.

5. **Volume Control:** Acoustics matter. High ceilings and concrete floors can turn a great venue into an echo chamber. Verify music levels beforehand to avoid early exits due to unbearable noise. If the establishment insists on music playing during the event, have them play a tract or station that offers a smooth electronic jazz blend turned very low.

6. **AV/Audio Check:** Microphones and speakers are networking essentials. Confirm the venue provides them, or else pack a portable setup to amplify your voice. We purchased

a portable unit to bring to venues that did not offer a PA system.

7. **Venue Type Magic**: Bar and grill combos are networking gold— food and drinks all in one place. For bars sans grub, plan for outside food delivery.

Weather Wisdom: Don't freeze or fry your attendees. Patio venues are fabulous, but not in the dead of winter or the peak of summer. Climate consideration is key.

Create your marketing verticals: You will need a mixer name, a free email account, a flier, and a branded Facebook business page. You may also want to consider some of the following:

1. Creation of a Group page on FB
2. Creation of a Twitter account
3. Creation of an Instagram account
4. Create an email account (use free ones like Constant Contact or MailChimp)
5. Be creative and add whatever you think would enhance your mixers and marketing thereof.

For your flier, it will need the following:

1. Mixer Name
2. Mixer Date
3. Mixer Venue
4. Mixer Address
5. Mixer Sponsor Logos (with click-throughs)
6. Mixer Hosts and business names if space is available.

You create the style and the vibe of the flier. Once you are happy with it **DO NOT CHANGE IT**. This is the most-seen marketing piece and is instrumental in continuity and mixer attendance.

Selecting the perfect venue sets the tone for vibrant connections. Get this right, and your mixers will be the talk of the town!

* * *

Chapter 2 Five-Step Successful Plan of Action

1. Set a Strategic Mixer Calendar:

- Plan your mixers from January to October to avoid holiday clashes, granting a well-deserved break in November and December.

2. Venue Selection Savvy:

- Trendy and Intriguing: Choose venues that attract attention and exude an upscale vibe, if feasible for your budget.
- Newly Opened Buzz: Keep an eye on new establishments; they can unexpectedly draw larger crowds.
- Comfort and Capacity: Balance seating and standing room, ensuring a comfortable yet conducive networking environment.
- Size and Acoustics: Opt for spacious places with good acoustics to accommodate attendees comfortably without overwhelming noise levels.

3. Consistency Builds Reputation:

- Commit to a consistent schedule for your mixers—reliability fosters trust and continued interest from sponsors and attendees.
- Create your marketing verticals.

4. AV and Logistics Check:

- Audio Equipment: Confirm the venue provides a suitable audio setup or be prepared to bring your portable system.
- Venue Type Readiness: Choose a venue that suits your event type— bar and grill venues are convenient for food and beverages.

5. Weather Considerations:

- Be mindful of the climate when selecting venues, especially those with outdoor space. Ensure it aligns with the comfort of your attendees.

Adhering to this checklist sets the foundation for a successful mixer, ensuring the right venue, schedule, and logistics for a fruitful networking experience.

3

Event Marketing Strategy

"Planning a mixer is like finding the perfect dance partner—you've got to pick the right day to avoid stepping on anyone's toes! Trust me, you don't want your event competing with a Chamber of Commerce mixer on the same evening. It's like crashing someone else's party with your hors d'oeuvres! Not the best networking strategy!"

Event Marketing Strategy Crafting a successful mixer requires meticulous research into industry-related commitments that may vie for your attendees' and sponsors' time. For instance, in the real estate sector, our mixer faced competition from a multitude of local and regional events hosted by industry players like Real Estate Brokers, Mortgage, and Title companies. Conducting comprehensive research minimizes competition and ensures a well-attended gathering.

    Calendar Considerations Date Matters: The day of your mixer holds immense significance. Avoid scheduling conflicts with concurrent events that might draw your target audience. For instance:

- **Title Companies and MLS Boards**: Frequent sponsors of day and evening events.

- **Chamber of Commerce:** Beware of their active monthly evening mixers; they can significantly impact attendance.
- **Mortgage Companies and Churches:** Host various day and evening events that might coincide with your mixer.

Research for the Perfect Timing Understand your attendees' industries and peruse their affiliate partners' calendars. Scrutinize charity events, church gatherings, and other entities known to host conflicting events. Consolidate this data to pinpoint the optimal day for your mixer.

The Time Slot Solution We opted for a concise 2-hour duration, starting promptly at 5:30 and concluding at 7:30. Respecting everyone's time is paramount. Our chosen window allowed venues to extend their happy hours till 7:30, an added draw for attendees. Anticipate early arrivals, so prepare to open the venue at least 15 minutes before the scheduled time.

Date and Time Confirmation Once you settle on a date and time **DO NOT CHANGE IT!** Remain consistent. Your venues need to plan and prepare for your event. Your sponsor needs to add it to their calendars as well. You will find over time that you will use your favorite venues 2-3 times a year. They will want to add your event to their event book. You will become a valued and appreciated source of income for them.

* * *

Chapter 3 Five-Step Successful Plan of Action

1. Research and Navigate Industry Calendars:

- Identify Competing Events: Scout for overlapping events hosted by affiliates in your attendees' industries, such as real estate boards, title companies, or chambers of commerce.
- Aggregate Information: Gather data from various sources, including affiliate websites and local entities, to avoid scheduling conflicts.

2. Date Selection Precision:

- Avoid Competing Events: Choose a date that minimizes competition from other industry-related gatherings to ensure a good turnout.
- Consider Affiliated Events: Consider events hosted by churches, charities, or other entities that might draw your target audience away.

3. Timing is Crucial:

- Concise Mixer Duration: Opt for a focused time frame, like a 2-hour event, respecting attendees' time commitments.
- Strategic Start and End Times: Commence and conclude promptly, starting at 5:30 and ending at 7:30, leveraging venue extensions for happy hours.

4. Venue Preparation and Early Arrival:

- Early Access Readiness: Prepare for early arrivals, ensuring the venue is accessible at least 15 minutes before the scheduled start.
- Venue Benefits: Seek venues that can extend happy hours or offer incentives to enhance attendee experience and engagement.

5. Thorough Planning through Research:

- Comprehensive Industry Insights: Dive deep into industry calendars, affiliate websites, and local events to strategically plan your mixer date and time.
- Collaborative Research: Engage with affiliates and partners to cross-reference calendars for potential conflicts and optimal scheduling.

Adhering to this checklist ensures meticulous planning, strategic scheduling, and maximum attendance, setting the stage for a successful and well-attended mixer event.

4

Sponsors and Partnerships

"Sponsors are like the VIP guests at your mixer—treating them well ensures the party never stops and the connections keep flowing!"

Sponsors and Partnerships Understanding the role of sponsors and how to engage them effectively is pivotal for the success of your mixer. Here's a breakdown of essential aspects regarding sponsorship:

Defining Sponsors and their Significance Sponsors, crucial for fostering connections and mutual benefit, are industry representatives seeking networking opportunities with your attendees. As a real estate-focused mixer, our sponsorship model included representatives from:

- Mortgage Lenders
- Real Estate Brokers
- Architects
- Insurance Agencies
- Appraisers
- Surveyors
- Bank Officers

- Developers
- Home Builders
- Home Warranty Companies
- Title Companies
- Home Inspectors
- Building Trades (e.g., Plumbers, Painters, etc.)

Engaging Sponsors Strategically

- **Initiating Sponsorship**: Actively seek potential sponsors through direct engagement, discussing the benefits of their involvement and presenting detailed statistics regarding the mixer's reach and impact. Maintain a continuous effort in marketing the mixer, ensuring sponsors see its value.
- **Determining Sponsorship Count**: The number of sponsors correlates with venue costs. Dividing the expenses equitably among sponsors, without showing favoritism, ensures fairness and avoids conflicts. Four is the sponsor's sweet spot! More than four sponsors on the stage can get crowded.

Sponsors Based on Venue Cost: Cost of Venue: If the total cost for the venue (inclusive of food and beverage) amounts to $600.00 (prices will change due to inflation)

Sponsorship Options:

- 3 Sponsors: At $200 sponsor fee each, totaling $600.
- 4 Sponsors: At $150 sponsor fee each, totaling $600.
- 2 Sponsors: At $300 sponsor fee each, totaling $600

Fairness and Equal Division:

- Equitable Split: To ensure fairness, divide the sponsorship fees equally among the sponsors. This practice avoids any appearance of favoritism and maintains credibility with sponsors.

Rule of Fairness:

- Avoid Favoritism: It's crucial never to display favoritism among sponsors, as this can quickly erode your credibility as an event organizer. Do not have competing industry sponsors on the stage at the same time unless they are friends and don't mind. I had two mortgage lenders sponsor the same mixer and the only reason we allowed it is because *they* thought it would be fun and wanted to do it.

- Only allow sponsors five minutes each to talk about their business. Any more than 20 minutes and your audience will start to leave and that is not good. Sponsors will have problems speaking in front of people and will ask to use props or audio-visual tools. We did not allow it. Some sponsors would use alcohol to get some "liquid courage." Watch the sponsors who'll utilize alcohol as they can get "windy" and you will have to move them along if they run over their five minutes. You will always be watched by the current sponsors and future sponsors on your equitable handling of them.

- By using these fee divisions based on the venue cost and ensuring equal distribution of sponsorship fees, you maintain fairness and avoid any perception of bias, fostering a balanced an impartial sponsorship model for your mixers.

Providing Sponsorship Value:

Offer sponsors a range of benefits to ensure value for their sponsorship fees. These include:

- Detailed metrics on email marketing reach, click rates, and post-mixer attendee lists were provided within 24 hours of the event.
- Online and offline marketing collateral featuring their branding and hyperlinks.
- Opportunities for personal connections and introductions within their target industries.
- Expectations from Sponsors: Sponsors are expected to pay their proportional share, arrive on time, bring business cards and marketing collateral, present a brief 3–5-minute business talk, and actively engage in networking during the event.
- Efficient Communication and Payment: Communicate promptly with sponsors regarding event details and deadlines. Prioritize collecting proportional shares well before the event, ensuring sponsors are committed and engaged.

Enhancing Sponsorship Experience

To elevate sponsorship value, provide digital event fliers with sponsor branding, facilitate Facebook marketing with backlinks to

their business pages, live stream events, or take pictures during the event and post them to Facebook or your favorite social media platform.

Continuously brainstorm new strategies to amplify their investment returns. Remember, sponsors are the lifeblood of your mixers and most of them are small business owners that have little marketing experience or no time to market themselves and their business. The mixer provides them with that opportunity. Treating them fairly and responsibly not only ensures their renewal but also transforms them into valuable lead generators.

Chapter 4 Five-Step Successful Plan of Action

1. Strategic Sponsor Identification:

- Research & Outreach: Identify potential sponsors aligned with your mixer's industry. Engage in direct outreach, highlighting the benefits and value they can gain from participating.

2. Tailored Sponsorship Counts:

- Equitable Division: Determine sponsorship counts based on venue costs. Ensure fairness by dividing fees equally among sponsors without showing favoritism.

3. Value-Oriented Sponsorship Benefits:

- Detailed Sponsor Benefits: Offer sponsors a comprehensive package, including:
- Metrics on email marketing reach and click-through rates.
- Post-mixer attendee lists.
- Online and offline marketing with their branding and hyperlinks.
- Opportunities for targeted introductions and connections.

4. Clear Expectations & Communication:

- Set Expectations: Communicate sponsor responsibilities—timely payment, attendance, bringing marketing collateral, and delivering a brief business talk.
- Efficient Communication: Maintain timely communication, sharing event details, deadlines, and marketing collateral

promptly.

5. Continuous Sponsorship Enhancement:

• Constant Value Addition: Consistently innovate and enhance sponsorship benefits.

• Provide digital event fliers featuring sponsor branding.

• Facilitate Facebook marketing with backlinks to their business pages.

• Continuously brainstorm new strategies to elevate their investment returns.

Adopting these steps ensures a strategic and engaging approach to sponsors, fostering a mutually beneficial relationship that enhances their investment and maximizes the success of your mixers.

5

Marketing Budget

"Planning a mixer's budget is a bit like hosting a potluck—choose the best ingredients within your means, and everyone leaves with a full belly and a smile! Just without the risk of someone bringing a Jello mold surprise."

Marketing Budget Once your venue and event date are set, it's time to create a comprehensive budget for your mixer.

Key Considerations for Budgeting:

- **Projected Attendance**: Estimate the number of attendees—typically ranging from 30 to 100—to establish a preliminary budget framework.
- **Venue Costs:** Inquire about additional event fees beyond food and beverage. Ensure clarity on the per-head charges for food and beverage. For instance, if the venue charges $20 per head for food and beverage and you have 50 guests, the total cost amounts to $1000. We typically had four sponsors at $300 each, resulting in a $1200 mixer budget.

Bar Management Discussions:

- Liquor and Beverage Choices: Discuss beverage options with the bar manager, focusing on cost-effective choices like well liquors, domestic beers, and budget-friendly wines. Premium alcohol might exceed your budget unless offered at a discount by the venue.

Food Selection and Arrangements:

- Menu Planning: Collaborate with the bar manager at least three weeks before the mixer to finalize food and beverage selections. Ensure a classy menu within your budget.
- Contract Signing: Confirm menu choices and ensure tips for bartenders are included in the contract before signing.
- Alternate Food Arrangements: If utilizing venues where outside food is allowed, coordinate with sponsors for food payments and vendor arrangements. Always clarify payment methods and expectations with the venue manager.

Payment Method and Responsibility:

- Payment Handling: Discuss payment methods with the venue— sponsors can pay separately via credit card, check, or cash during the event.
- Financial Responsibility: Never underwrite the mixer personally or expect your business to do so. Avoid situations where cost overruns fall on you unexpectedly.

Menu Suggestions for Cost-Efficiency:

- **Food Selection:**

  - Opt for 3-4 hearty appetizers that go a long way, such as chips, salsa, queso, and poppers, or cost-effective options like Fajitas. Pizza is okay but it must be large and priced effectively.
  - If you are bringing in food Mexican food is the way to go! Fajitas, rice, and beans with all the fixings are the easiest and most cost-effective way of providing food for your mixer.
  - Providing pizzas is a good option too, but it is also a lot less appealing seeing opened boxes of pizzas on a table and the attendees serving themselves from the boxes.

Beverage Choices: Consider cost-effective selections to manage the most significant part of the budget—alcohol expenses. Stick to "well" liquors, domestic beers, and reasonably priced wines to control costs.

Pricing Considerations: Set price ranges for various beverages:

- Wine: $6-$8 per glass
- Margaritas (if available): $5-$6 per glass
- Domestic Beer: $3-$4 per bottle
- Craft Beer: $4-$5 per bottle/glass
- Well Liquor: $6 per glass (Prices subject to inflation adjustments)
- Happy Hour Extension: If possible, negotiate with the venue to extend happy hour pricing, maximizing your budget's impact.

Financial Responsibility & Payment Handling:
- Ensure sponsors pay separately via preferred payment methods—credit card, check, or cash—directly to the venue during the event. arrangements with sponsors for the food and vendor setup.
- Establish clear payment methods and expectations with the venue manager.

* * *

Chapter 5 Five-Step Successful Plan of Action

1. Venue & Attendance Estimation
- Select an appropriate venue considering projected attendance (30-100).
- Clarify venue costs—ensure clear per-head charges for food and beverage.

2. Bar Management Discussions:

- Engage with the bar manager to discuss beverage choices—prioritize cost-effective options like well liquors, domestic beers, and budget-friendly wines.
- Negotiate happy hour extensions to maximize the budget's impact.

3. Menu Planning & Contract Signing:

- Collaborate with the venue's bar manager at least three weeks before the event to finalize the food and beverage menu within the budget.
- Ensure contract clauses cover the agreed-upon menu and include tips for bartenders.

4. Alternate Food Arrangements (if applicable):

- If utilizing venues allowing outside food, coordinate payment arrangements with sponsors for the food and vendor setup.

- Establish clear payment methods and expectations with the venue manager.

5. Financial Responsibility & Payment Handling:

- Ensure sponsors pay separately via preferred payment methods - credit card, check, or cash paid directly to the venue during the event.
- Avoid personally underwriting the mixer or expecting your business to do so to prevent unexpected cost overruns.

This checklist serves as a concise guide to cover critical aspects—venue selection, menu planning, financial responsibility, and sponsor coordination—for a successful and financially sound mixer event.

6

Mixer Branding and Promotional

"Building a successful mixer is like crafting a masterpiece - it begins with a stroke of creativity in naming, branding, and setting the stage for an unforgettable event!"

Your Brand Matters:

As soon as the present mixer was over, I would go to work the next day on next month's mixer promotion. I would input all the business cards and sign-in sheets collected from the night before and add them to create the Sponsors spreadsheet for integration into their marketing verticals and then I would merge the sponsor spreadsheet into our spreadsheet. I had six columns on both spreadsheets.

Column 1 First and Last Name
Column 2 Category (Realtors®, lender, banker, etc.)
Column 3 Position of attendee
Column 4 Company of attendees
Column 5 Contact Name (if different than attendee)
Column 6 Email Address

I would then add the business cards into a large binder with clear business card sheets. The cards were organized like the spreadsheet above. This became a very handy tool when a sponsor would call me to ask for an introduction at the next mixer. Most of the Realtor cards had pictures of themselves on them and I would use them a lot.

Developing Your Mixer Brand:

By this chapter, you should have developed your mixer name, brand, and logo for marketing purposes. If you are creative, you can do this yourself using <u>Canva.com</u>. It's free and you can make everything you need for marketing fliers there. All you'll need for marketing is an 8 x 10 flier. It needs to be digital. You will need a hard copy for reproduction to give to your less-than-internet-savvy sponsors. I would usually drop 10 off to the future sponsors who needed them. For the other sponsors, I would send a digital copy.

Online Creatives:
Create a Facebook business page.
Create a Group page on FB
Create a Twitter account.
Create an Instagram account.
Create an email account (use free ones like <u>MailChimp</u>)

Be creative and add whatever you think would enhance your mixers and marketing thereof.

* * *

Chapter 6 Five-Step Successful Plan of Action

1. Define Mixer Identity:

- Choose a catchy and relevant mixer name that resonates with your target audience.
- Create a free email account dedicated to the mixer to maintain professional correspondence.

2. Develop Promotional Materials:

- Design an eye-catching digital flier:
- Include essential details: Mixer Name, Date, Venue, Address, and Sponsor Logos with clickable links.
- Highlight hosts' business names if space permits.
- Craft a consistent style and tone that reflects the event's vibe. Once finalized, refrain from altering it for consistency.

3. Establish Online Presence:

- Set up a branded Facebook business page to showcase the mixer and engage with potential attendees.
- Consider creating a Group page on Facebook to foster a community around your mixer.
- Establish a presence on Twitter and Instagram to expand your reach and engage with a wider audience.
- Create an email account using platforms like Constant Contact or Mailchimp to manage communication effectively.

4. Enhance Marketing Endeavors:

- Explore additional creative avenues:
- Incorporate innovative ideas to enhance the overall marketing of the mixers.
- Consider using creative strategies or platforms that align with your audience preferences and enhance mixer promotion.

5. Ensure Consistency and Continuity:

- Maintain the integrity of your marketing materials and online presence:
- Consistently utilize the same flier design and messaging for enhanced recognition.
- Regularly update and engage with your social media platforms to sustain interest and attendance for future mixers.

This plan focuses on establishing a strong and consistent brand presence while utilizing various digital platforms for effective mixer promotion and engagement.

7

Building Your Email List

"Networking wisdom: Turn your mixer invites into VIP passes, collect business cards with finesse, and remember, sharing your email list is like giving away the secret sauce—best kept to spice up your mixers, not someone else's cocktail party!"

Effective networking extends beyond the event night. Here are two proven strategies to build and utilize an impactful email list for your mixers:

Method 1: No More Cold Calling - Now You Can Get Past The Front Desk

Engage personally with potential attendees by turning your mixer invitation into a welcome offering. Here's how it's done:

- **Personal Invitations**: This was my favorite marketing hack. I would always keep a handful of fliers in my car and as I was out doing personal or business errands, I'd inevitably stumble upon an enterprise that appeared to align seamlessly with our industry sectors and had yet to participate in our mixers.

I would walk into the establishment and offer a flier invitation to our mixer and voilà the front desk person melted in my hands!

- **Permission and Collection:** While I was in the establishment, I would politely request permission to collect business cards that were displayed. I was never told no. This marketing method is quite effective and often met with enthusiasm and is also a great conversation starter. Keep in mind, that you're extending invitations, not making *solicitations*, and in return, providing significant value. Tap into the potential of this highly efficient strategy for building your contact list. As your list grows, so does the value for sponsors, presenting excellent opportunities for marketing backlinks, impressions, and a consistent flow of attendees to each monthly mixer. The result? A positive impact on the overall growth of your mixers

Method 2: Post Mixer List Generation After the mixer concludes, here's how to effectively manage and utilize the gathered business cards the next day:

- **Post Mixer Collection**: Compile all collected business cards and sign-up sheets into a dedicated email list exclusively for the sponsors of the previous night's mixer.
- **Sponsor Marketing Tools**: Share this list with your sponsors the next day, providing them with a valuable marketing resource to directly engage with attendees within 24 hours.
- **Demographic Insights**: Accompany the list with a breakdown of attendees and their respective categories, offering valuable insights into attendee demographics.

- **Publicly express gratitude:** to the sponsors via multiple channels, including email and social media.

Purposeful Invitations: Target invites from specific industry demographics, ensuring a well-balanced attendance at your mixers. For instance, prioritize inviting Realtors® if they align with your mixer's demographics to enhance networking opportunities. Lenders love Realtors® and it was always a delicate balance to bring in new Realtors® without the mixer being weighted to Lenders and Realtors® only.

- **Strategic List Categorization:** How you categorize your email list holds immense importance for future use. Organize it thoughtfully, considering attendee demographics and sponsor preferences to maximize engagement.

You may encounter requests to share or sell your valuable master list, often tempting due to its targeted marketing potential. However, I strongly advise against such actions. Sharing or selling your list could tarnish your credibility and significantly devalue your standing in your market.

Building your email list is just the beginning. Purposeful categorization and prompt sharing with sponsors amplify the networking impact of your mixers while fostering meaningful connections for all involved.

* * *

Chapter 7 Five Step Successful Plan of Action

1. Pre-Mixer Preparation

- Design visually appealing and exclusive invitations that resemble party invites.
- Create permission slips to accompany the invitations, clearly stating the benefits of sharing business cards.
- Train your team on the art of inviting rather than soliciting, emphasizing the value proposition.

2. Engaging at the Mixer

- Foster a friendly atmosphere, encouraging attendees to see the mixer as an exclusive gathering.
- Ensure that your team effectively communicates the value of being on the email list.

3. Post Mixer Collection and Compilation

- Promptly collect all gathered business cards after the mixer.
- Create a dedicated email list for sponsors, organizing it based on attendee categories.
- Double-check for accuracy and completeness of the contact information before sharing.

4. Empowering Sponsors

- Share the compiled list with sponsors the day after the mixer.
- Emphasize the time-sensitive nature of the information and the value it provides for direct engagement.
  - Include demographic insights to help sponsors tailor their marketing approaches.

5. Strategic Use and Maintenance

- Categorize the email list thoughtfully based on attendee demographics and sponsor preferences.
- Regularly update the list with new contacts from each mixer.
- Emphasize the importance of ethical use and discourage any attempts to share or sell the master list.

Remember, the success of your plan relies on the seamless execution of each step and maintaining a genuine, value-driven approach throughout the process. Happy mixing!

8

The Mixer Experience

"Hosting a mixer is like throwing a party for professionals—where the dress code is business casual, and the only drama allowed is in the networking. So, buckle up your socializing shoes, because in this chapter, we're turning handshakes into connections and business cards into VIP passes. Let the mixing (and maybe a little shaking) begin!"

Pre-Mixer Logistics:

Financial Preparedness:

- Ensure sponsor checks are made payable to the venue and have them ready for the manager.
- Confirm the food and drink menu upon arrival, considering the option of the bar manager printing the drink menu.
- Have tabletops printed in advance and place on tables

Arrival and Setup:

Early Arrival and Sponsor Interaction:

Prepare color-coded tickets for efficient billing. Use two-sided tickets. We used to use two colors. Red for example is for wine or liquor tickets and white is for beer tickets.

We allowed two drink tickets per person. Always keep one half of the ticket for the raffle basket and the other half goes to attendees for drinks. Note: decline to give tickets without a sign-in or business card. Your sponsors want to know who has attended for their marketing purposes.

- Arrive one hour early to handle pre-mixer issues. There will always be some!
- Confirm the PA system is functioning or set up your portable system.
- Ensure sponsors have arrived and guide them to pay their share promptly.
- Collect raffle gifts from sponsors for later use.
- Be mindful of sponsor-desired connection requests.
- Distribute tabletop swag from sponsors and place them on the tables.
- Assemble the greeting table.

Greeting Table Setup:

- Cover the table with a tablecloth.
- Set up a basket for business card entries for prize drawings.
- Prepare a sign-up sheet for those without business cards.
- Provide pens and name tags for attendee sign-ins.
- Have a business card holder for sponsor cards.
- Bring a tablecloth for the presentation. Set the table up as far away from the entry door as possible. The door will get clogged for the first 15 minutes and could disrupt the flow of attendees into the venue.

Guests Arrival and Engagement:

- Greet attendees warmly, especially those arriving early and alone. I would always make sure the ones who were alone stayed along my side until more people came and then I would introduce them to others.

"I watched over the years a once shy female attendee turned into a networking ninja at our mixers and in the larger community. Who knew a simple introduction and wine could be the secret sauce to her business success!"

- Encourage attendees to drop business cards in the basket or fill out the signup sheet.
- Distribute drink tickets corresponding to business cards.
- Briefly explain the serving situation and guide guests to food.
- Coordinate with your partner on the table and crowd interaction.

During the Mixer:

Maintaining Professionalism and Control:

- Please don't drink alcohol during the event. Hosts don't get drunk to maintain their credibility. Remember sponsors and future sponsors are watching your behavior and deciding if they want to invest in you and your mixer.

- Ensure a well-organized sponsor introduction and raffle gift presentation.

- Gather the sponsors at 6:45 pm on stage and allow them to each speak for five minutes. Have them each draw a business card from the raffle basket after speaking, introduce the winner, and have the winner come up to accept the gift and move on to the next sponsor.

• By 7:05 pm the sponsors should be done speaking and the drawing for raffle gifts is over. Thank the sponsors and inform the audience of next month's mixer. By 7:10 pm the attendees typically start to leave. Your mixer at this point still has 20 minutes left. We developed another raffle that was presented by our company. At 7:30 pm we would have a $100 cash prize raffle. This stopped the audience from leaving and it was a fun and great way to end the mixer as well as great advertising for our company. It's your mixer be creative to keep guests until the end.

Post-Mixer:

Final Drawings and Closing:

• Conduct the final drawing at 7:30, expressing gratitude and announcing the next mixer's location.
• Settle the tab with the manager, being financially responsible for any overages.

After-Mixer Mixer and Cleanup:

• Allow guests to stay and enjoy themselves after 7:30. This is the time the venue gets to make additional revenue from the "holdovers" from the mixer.
• Hosts clean up tables, gather marketing materials, and store them for repeat sponsors.

- Engage with attendees, seek feedback, and discuss improvements.
- Emphasize the importance of constructive criticism for continual improvement.

Remember, the success of your mixer is not just about the event itself but also about the lasting impressions and connections it leaves. Enjoy the post-mixer moments and keep refining for an even better experience next time!

Use this space for notes after reading Chapter 8:

* * *

Chapter 8 Five Step Successful Plan of Action

1. Prelude Preparations

- **Financial Foundations**: Ensure sponsor checks are ready, payable to the venue.
- **Menu Mastery:** Confirm the food and drink menu upon arrival.
- **Print Perfection**: Have tabletops printed and ready for setup.

2. Early Arrival and Sponsor Interaction

- **Time is Key:** Arrive at least an hour early to tackle pre-mixer challenges.
- **Financial Facilitation:** Ensure sponsors arrive and smoothly pay their share.
- **Gift Gathering:** Collect raffle gifts from sponsors for later use.
- **Strategic Networking**: Be attentive to sponsor-desired connections as you navigate the room.
- **Setup Perfection:** Distribute tabletops and set up the greeting table.
- **Colorful Coding:** Prepare color-coded tickets for efficient billing.

3. Greeting Table

- **Basket for Bliss:** Set up a basket for business card entries for prize drawings.
- **Sign-Up Savvy:** Prepare a sign-up sheet for those sans business cards.
- **Tool Kit:** Provide pens and name tags for smooth attendee sign-ins.
- **Business Card Haven:** Have a dedicated holder for sponsor business cards.
- **Visual Appeal:** Bring a tablecloth for an aesthetically pleasing presentation.

4. Guests Arrival and Engagement

- **Warm Welcomes**: Greet attendees warmly, especially those arriving early and solo.
- **Card Conundrum:** Encourage attendees to drop business cards or fill out the signup sheet.
- **Drink Tickets**: Distribute drink tickets corresponding to business cards.
- **Serving Wisdom:** Briefly explain the serving situation and guide guests to the food.
- **Collaborative Coordination**: Coordinate with your partner on table and crowd interaction.

5. During and Post-Mixer Mastery

- **Host Sobriety:** Hosts don't get drunk—maintain your credibility and professionalism.
- **Mic Magic:** Ensure a well-organized sponsor introduction and raffle gift presentation.

- **Incentive Insight**: Create an incentive to keep guests until the end, such as a cash giveaway.
- **Schedule Mastery**: Stick to the schedule with mic announcements at 6:45 and 7:30.
- **Graceful Goodbye:** After the final drawing, express gratitude, announce the next event, and settle the tab with the manager.
- **Post-Party Protocol:** Allow guests to linger for an after-mixer mixer. Clean up thoughtfully, gather marketing materials, and engage with attendees for feedback and improvement ideas.

With these five steps, you'll not only host a successful mixer but also create a networking experience that leaves a lasting impression on all attendees! Cheers to mastering the mix!

9

Conclusion

"Mixers aren't just about shaking cocktails; they're about stirring genuine connections that last longer than your favorite blend. So, is hosting mixers worth it? Absolutely! Because, let's face it, real handshakes beat virtual likes any day."

Nurturing Business through Genuine Connections Is the effort of hosting mixers worth it? Undoubtedly so. The relationships fostered, both personal and professional, during our two-year tenure of hosting mixers were invaluable to our business growth. Within our construction business, we aimed to cultivate enduring business affiliations, particularly within our industry's preferred partnerships. Through these mixers, pivotal connections were forged:

- **Discovery of Essential Partners:** The mixer platform introduced me to vital entities in our field—my mortgage lender, appraiser, and surveyor—all key figures found through this networking endeavor.
- **Solidifying Business Ties:** Notably, my partnerships with the title company escrow officer, banker, and insurance professional were solidified through these mixers. These relationships, singular in their form, sustained a consistent flow of business for

numerous fruitful years until we decided to retire early and relocate out of state.

Reflecting on this journey, it's crucial to consider a fundamental shift:

- **From Artificial to Authentic:** This book advocates for a shift away from artificial online connections, emphasizing the creation of a community founded on genuine interactions—smiles, handshakes, and direct one-on-one business relationships nurtured through the art of networking.

In closing, I urge the reader, leveraging the guidance offered within this book, to contemplate the immense value of moving beyond the digital facade and embracing the power of face-to-face connections, paving the way for enduring and impactful business relationships.

If you found this book helpful, I'd be very appreciative if you left a favorable review for the book on Amazon!